EMBRACING ACTION

Overcoming the Fear of Failure, Procrastination, and Perfectionism

Dr. Donald J. Henry

Table of Contents

Disclaimer

Book Description

Do you ever find yourself teetering on the edge of a new adventure, with hopes and dreams flashing in your eyes, but the constant worry that you won't be good enough keeps you from starting it? Or on the other hand, perhaps you've felt the gravitational draw of lingering, that tricky friend that baits you away from the errands you realize you ought to handle.

What's more, we should not disregard the hard-to-find journey for flawlessness, that illusion of perfection that occasionally holds us back from venturing out.
Guess what, then? You are not alone, and you certainly are not destined to remain trapped in this whirlpool of self-doubt and inaction for the rest of your life.

"Embracing Action: Overcoming the Fear of Failure, Procrastination, and Perfectionism" is here to direct you through the maze of these normal difficulties, offering a well-disposed hand to assist you with breaking liberated from your grip.

In this charming excursion, you'll jump profound into the brain research behind these road obstructions, uncovering the underlying foundations of your apprehension about disappointment, the tricky ways tarrying creeps in, and the legends that have sustained the way of life of hairsplitting.

But don't worry; this isn't just another self-help book that promises nothing.
A compass directs you to an activity-situated outlook, a mentality that engages you to transform goals into substantial outcomes.

Prepare to Release Your True Capacity

With warmth and knowledge, every part takes you by the hand and strolls you through the most common way of changing these difficulties into venturing stones. You'll gain the ability to change your perspective and see failure as a path to growth rather than a stumbling block.
You'll find the wizardry of developing strength, the specialty of defining reachable objectives, and the force of adjusting your activities to your qualities.

But that's not all, you'll also learn how to overcome procrastination, silence your inner perfectionist, and develop a proactive plan of action that moves you forward. You'll learn to persevere through the inevitable bumps in the road and get past them. Furthermore, as you venture through these pages, you'll end up enlivened by the genuine accounts of those who've transformed disappointment into fuel for their prosperity.

Your Journey Begins Here. Are you prepared to embark on a life-changing journey? With "Embracing Action," you're not simply perusing a book you're leaving on an excursion of self-revelation, development, and strengthening. You'll be furnished with instruments, bits of knowledge, and a recently discovered point of view that will engage you to step intensely into the existence you imagine.

Whether you're a visionary looking to transform your dreams into the real world, an objective setter prepared to handle difficulties head-on, or somebody burnt out on the loss of motion of hairsplitting, this book is your guide to embracing activity and releasing your maximum capacity.

Prepare to turn the page, leap, and begin your journey toward a life of purpose, progress, and the joy of accepting imperfect, beautifully authentic action.
Your experience is standing by.

Introduction

In the grand theatre of life, we frequently find ourselves watching the spotlight on the centre stage from behind the stage with a mix of longing and fear. A universal human desire is to act, to step into the spotlight, and to leave our mark. However, again and again, we are kept down by an undetectable power: the deadening grasp of inaction.

Preparing the Scene: The Loss of Motion of Inaction

Picture a material overflowing with potential, trusting that the craftsman's brush will rejuvenate it. Likewise, our lives are materials anticipating the strokes of our activities to make energetic and significant encounters. However, just like a painter confronting a blank canvas, our fear of not getting it "just right" can overwhelm us. Perfectionism, the fear of failing, and the tempting trap of procrastination are all manifestations of this fear.

The Power of Embracing Action

Amid skepticism and hesitation, the power of embracing action shines like a beacon of empowerment. Activity is the power that changes expectations into the real world, dreams into accomplishments. It is the cure to the incapacitating impacts of hairsplitting, the apprehension about disappointment, and the grip of dawdling. We rewrite the script of our lives and become the authors of our narratives by taking deliberate steps forward. In this investigation, we will set out on an excursion to grasp the multifaceted dance between the apprehension about disappointment, tarrying, and the quest for flawlessness.

We will uncover the instruments that drive these examples of inaction, and all the more significantly, we will outfit ourselves with the devices and bits of knowledge to break liberated from their grip. Together, we will find the significant freedom that comes from embracing activity flawed, yet amazingly intense. Are you prepared to enter the transformation stage? Let's get out of the way of inaction and bravely enter the spotlight of progress.

Chapter 1

Figuring Out The

Feeling of Dread Toward Failure

In the maze of human feelings, the feeling of dread toward disappointment remains as an imposing sentinel, protecting the entry to our yearnings and dreams. An inclination can stop our advancement, dissolve our fearlessness, and shape our way of living. To beat this unavoidable trepidation, we should set out on an excursion to grasp its mind-boggling subtleties, following its starting points, and at last changing it into a power for development and strengthening.

Failure's Psychology: Causes and Repercussions

 Failure, in its many manifestations, carries a weight that is greater than its apparent impact. The brain science of disappointment is an intricate interaction of mental, close-to-home, and social cycles. A fundamental need for approval and validation is often at the heart of the fear of failure.

The possibility of missing the mark compromises our healthy identity worth and triggers an outpouring of feelings, from disgrace and humiliation to uneasiness and self-question. In turn, these emotional responses can cause us to steer clear of difficulties and take the shortest route.

The fear of failing has far-reaching effects. It can appear as hesitation, hairsplitting, or even aversion to chances that hold potential for development. Chronic stress and burnout can result from striving for an unattainable standard of perfection driven by the fear of failing.

As we explore the complicated scene of disappointment's brain science, we gain knowledge of the hidden causes that lead to this strong inclination.

Following the Starting points: Childhood, Society, and Self-Expectations

To truly comprehend the fear of failure, we must exhume its roots, which frequently delve deeply into our early childhood soil. Youth encounters assume a vital part in molding our convictions about progress, disappointment, and our capacities. Our perception of failure is influenced by the praise or criticism we receive, the messages we internalize from caregivers and authority figures, and the cultural narratives we encounter.

Society, with its generally expected impossible norms of accomplishment, further sustains the anxiety toward disappointment. We are inundated with images of success and societal standards that set an impossible standard from an early age. Our sense of inadequacy is exacerbated by the fear of not measuring up which drives the constant comparison to other people.

Also, the assumptions we place upon ourselves can become favorable places for apprehension about disappointment. The quest for flawlessness, while respectable in its expectations, can change into a tenacious disciplinarian, directing everything we might do and smothering our imagination.
As we follow the complicated snare of impacts that add to the apprehension about disappointment, we enlighten the way toward destroying its hold.

Moving Points of View: Considering Inability to be an Impetus for Growth

Amid the shadows of the apprehension about disappointment lies a desert spring of change. Moving our viewpoint on disappointment is much the same as speculative chemistry it transforms what was once incapacitating into a wellspring of strengthening.
Embracing disappointment as an impetus for development requires a key change in the way we see both achievement and difficulties.

At the point when we view disappointment through an alternate focal point, we remember it as an instructor as opposed to a victimizer. Failure becomes an essential component of success because it provides us with valuable information, lessons, and insights that help us move forward.
Resilience, adaptability, and a willingness to take calculated risks are all developed when failure is approached with a growth mindset.

In the following chapter, we will discuss the process of shifting perspectives in greater depth and offer practical methods for reassessing failure. We begin a transformative journey toward embracing failure as an essential stepping stone on the path to self-discovery and accomplishment by comprehending the psychology that underpins the fear of failure, tracing its origins, and adopting a transformative viewpoint.

Chapter 2

Untangling the Mysteries of

Procrastination

Few phenomena in human behavior are as pervasive and mysterious as procrastination. This chapter is an expedition into the core of procrastination, aiming to reveal its underlying causes, reveal its intricate mechanisms, and offer a path out of its clutches. We gain insight that enables us to turn avoidance into action as we solve the procrastination puzzle.

Demystifying Procrastination:
Basic Variables and Mechanisms

Hesitation, frequently excused as simple sluggishness or absence of self-control, is a multi-layered conduct with roots that dive profoundly into our mental and close-to-home scene. Underneath its silly outside lie complex mental elements and systems.

One key component is the human propensity to focus on momentary prizes over long-haul objectives, driven by the mind's multifaceted award framework.

Anxiety toward disappointment and compulsiveness, close mates of stalling, entwine to wind around a trap of evasion. The nervousness of not satisfying high guidelines can prompt deferment, as can the distress of confronting obscure or dubious results.

A foundation for addressing procrastination at its core is provided by an understanding of the interaction of these psychological factors.

The Connection Between Procrastination and Perfectionism

Despite their apparent disparity, procrastination and perfectionism have a profound connection that can fuel a cycle of inaction. Procrastination is used as a means of defending against the possibility of failure as a result of the overwhelming and paralyzing effects of perfectionism's unwavering pursuit of perfection. The quest for a romanticized result turns into a blockade against making blemished strides.

However, this association likewise holds the way to unwinding the stalling puzzle. By tending to compulsiveness and rethinking outcomes in additional versatile ways, we can debilitate the bonds that attach delay to the apprehension about not having the goods.

The excursion toward beating lingering is unpredictably connected with developing self-sympathy and embracing the blemishes intrinsic to the innovative strategy.

Breaking the Cycle: Methodologies for Defeating Procrastination

As we stand at the junction of hesitation and efficiency, a huge number of procedures entice us toward a way of activity. From mental strategies that challenge twisted convictions and figured designs, to social intercessions that structure our current circumstance for progress, a rich tool stash is available to us.

The perilous terrain of avoidance is aided by time management strategies like the Two-Minute Rule and the Pomodoro Technique. Developing mindfulness and care, we figure out how to distinguish the triggers that move us toward tarrying and foster an elevated feeling of organization in diverting our concentration.

In addition, it is impossible to overstate the significance of accountability, support networks, and setting attainable objectives.
By embracing flaws and understanding that progress is brought into the world from predictable exertion, we change lingering from a hindrance into a venturing stone.

Why do I procrastinate?

1. You are genuinely connected to the result. You procrastinate when you are emotionally heightened. This will sound unreasonable, however, the more put you are in a result, the more noteworthy the desire to linger can be. Although this may appear to alleviate any anxiety you may be experiencing regarding the task, it is not always the case.

The brain's negative bias is to blame for this. In particular, regarding pessimistic, upsetting feelings, research has shown that the cerebrum distinguishes and stores gloomy feelings uniquely in contrast to good feelings. Accordingly, the apprehension about disappointment or apprehension about disheartening others bests the deep satisfaction, bliss, and fervor we hope to feel if and when we achieve something, making us delay and try not to get that result.

2. Hesitation turns into your reason
Procrastination is a great way to self-sabotage when our fear of failure causes us to want to succeed. While we are stalling, there is a piece of our mindfulness that knows that on the off chance that we don't get along nicely, we can put it on the way that we needed more time.

Whether we are handling a major show for work or working on our wellness, we take comfort in the way that on the off chance that the result doesn't live up to our assumptions, we can perceive ourselves that it was an absence of time that wrecked us and not our inadequacy or deficiency.

3. You go through an analysis-paralysis process,
This particular sort of delaying stalls us out in the rumination stage. We let ourselves know that we rant for an additional contribution from others, to rest on the thought some more, or to consider it for a couple of additional days. In doing as such, we put things off endlessly, or, on account of undertakings that have a cutoff time, as late as possible.

At the point when we arrive at our cutoff time, we are presently confronted with a heap of work to sort and unload in record time. When we multitask, we become lost and feel even more stuck. On account of our fantasies, we might in all likelihood never start to pursue them; the more we delay, the more we lose the association and the assurance.

As we reduce most, if not all, connections with our desires, we move away from our motivation and can neglect to focus on who we are. We don't perceive the individual we find in the mirror since it has been ages since she made progress toward a truly amazing job or took part in one of her interests or side interests, like yoga, craftsmanship, kickboxing, or sewing!

4. Your previous encounters take care of the hesitation:
Assuming that you've invested energy in your life buckling down for practically no award, your previous encounters could affect your eagerness to hop in on new tasks. If so, you might have to do a stock of any educational encounters you have had around the objective finish.

Think back to your early years: at home or school, what sort of strain was put on you to put forth and accomplish objectives? How were your achievements celebrated versus how were your inadequacies rebuffed? If you can recognize that your best was rarely sufficient, you might have the option to see the reason why you will quite often try not to invest the energy now.

It's possible that you like to lie to yourself and say you didn't have enough time, or you may be afraid to start anything because you think you'll end up disappointing yourself or others.
When it comes to particular projects or tasks, any or all of the aforementioned factors could be the cause of our procrastination. Some of the time, we might encounter each of the four reasons when we are confronted with specific targets.

Along these lines, we might experience some difficulty handling each justification behind our delaying, finding that unloading one doesn't ease the other, and so forth.
For this situation, it is useful to attempt to rank your reasons arranged by significance and tackle them either from least important to move or the other way around.

Breaking them into pieces is a method for improving on the thing you are managing and executing the devices you have accessible to defeat your hesitation.

Ten (10) Methods for Combating Procrastination

1. Assume responsibility for your review space by concentrating on an area liberated from interruptions.

2. Create a "to-do" list.

3. Spread out a day-to-day practice.

4. Self-pay off and give yourself rewards. When I've finished reading these 10 pages 5, I can watch television for 30 minutes.

Partition and Overcoming diminish the apparent trouble of enormous errands by separating them into more modest ones. As you complete every single unit and progress forward toward the accompanying one in a matter of seconds, you'll be done.

6. To deal with your time, utilize an organizer.

7. Follow the 10-minute time limit. Right when you experience trouble getting everything moving, select a specific endeavor, similar to three pages of examining or "I will persevere through 10 minutes scrutinizing perpetually." Close to the completion of 10 minutes, see the sum you've done. Work for ten minutes at a time until you are satisfied with your progress.

8. Before giving up, do something else when the examination process is finished. Start another assignment; then you will be ahead when you plunk down to think again.

9. Convey cheat sheets, notes, and other audit materials with you so you can use your open time. While waiting for the bus, riding in a vehicle, standing in line, and so on, recall and review your notes.

10. Complete two things immediately. Unite recitation and review with another development. Present terms and definitions while you are running or having your lunch.

We will examine how to cultivate an action-oriented perspective that propels us forward in the upcoming chapter, which will delve into the art of shifting our mindset.
As we unwind the complicated strings of lingering, we open the possibility to recover our time, inventiveness, and the quest for significant achievements.

Chapter 3

The Myth Of Perfectionism

In a society that emphasizes perfection and success, the allure of perfectionism can be both appealing and deceptive. This part attempts to strip away the reflexive facade of hairsplitting, uncovering its different sorts and qualities, uncovering the secret cost it demands on our psychological well-being and prosperity, and at last, directing us toward a groundbreaking change in how we might interpret achievement and blemish.

Unmasking Perfectionism: Types and Characteristics

Perfectionism is a multifaceted idea that manifests itself in a variety of forms, each with its unique characteristics and manifestations. From self-arranged compulsiveness, portrayed by setting ridiculously high private principles, to socially endorsed hairsplitting, driven by outer tensions to adjust to apparent goals, the woven artwork of compulsiveness is complicated and nuanced.

Perfectionism's characteristics frequently manifest as both strengths and weaknesses. A strong commitment to quality, a drive for excellence, and meticulous attention to detail is often praised. In any case, these ethics can twist into pointless propensities, for example, persistent disappointment, a powerlessness to appoint, and an unwavering apprehension about disappointment. We can see how perfectionism affects our lives when its layers are revealed.

The Expensive Dangers of Perfectionism: Psychological Wellness and Well-Being

Underneath the veneer of impeccable achievement lies a secret expense that hairsplitting claims on our emotional wellness and prosperity. Research has shown that the quest for flawlessness is related to elevated degrees of nervousness, wretchedness, and stress.

The tenacious mission for an out-of-reach standard powers a voracious pattern of endeavoring, dissolving our confidence, and planting seeds of discontent.

The negative effects of perfectionism are felt in many different areas of life. Connections might endure as the quest for faultlessness generally rules out sympathy and understanding. Inventive undertakings might be smothered as the feeling of dread toward missing the mark subdues advancement and trial and error.

Perceiving the cost compulsiveness takes on our all-encompassing prosperity is a significant stage toward freedom.

Rethinking Achievement: Embracing Imperfection

A glimmer of hope emerges amid the devastation caused by perfectionism the possibility of redefining success and embracing imperfection. We free success from the chains of flawlessness by shifting our focus from external validation to intrinsic contentment.

By embracing flaws as a basic piece of the human experience, we discharge ourselves from the stifling grasp of impossible goals.

Redefining success turns it into a journey of self-discovery, development, and resilience. Embracing missteps and misfortunes as important illustrations, we manufacture a way toward a more significant and satisfying presence. The pursuit of excellence transforms into a dynamic dance that celebrates progress, no matter how small, from a strenuous ascent of an immovable peak.

In the parts ahead, we will dig into the most common way of moving our outlook and destroying the fussbudget system that frequently holds us hostage. As we expose the fantasy of compulsiveness, we uncover the potential for genuine self-articulation, inventiveness, and a significant feeling of achievement that rises above the restrictions of perfection.

Chapter 4

Accepting Failure As a Stepping Stone

In a society that is preoccupied with achievement and success, the idea of failure frequently appears to be an unwanted intruder. However, inside the domain of difficulties and frustrations lies a secret fortune: the possibility to change disappointment into a strong impetus for development and self-disclosure.

This section is an excursion into the core of embracing disappointment, investigating how to develop a development outlook, fabricate strength, and draw motivation from accounts of the individuals who have transformed disappointment into a take-off platform for progress.

Life is a journey filled with trials, failures, and successes.

To prevail without disappointment is interesting. What you ought to always have in your sub-conscience is that everybody bombs in without a doubt. The involvement with falling flat is smashing, yet it is possible that you face it or you go down with it.

I came to acknowledge the way that disappointment is a venturing stone to progress after attempting ordinarily to be what I need. Today I'm seeing that my disappointments were disappointments as well as an interesting and open door for me to realize what's genuinely going on with progress.

Fruitful individuals become what they are a direct result of how they answer their disappointments. Life is brimming with deterrents, nothing truly goes out effectively without snags. You alone need to choose whether to blame these hindrances for your disappointment or use them as a justification for your prosperity.

Fruitful individuals use them as a venturing stone to their prosperity. You will need to involve your disappointments as input into what you do. To decide to find actual success, you should be prepared to acknowledge disappointments. That you need to recognize because it is an essential part of making progress.

Developing a Development Outlook: Gaining from Setbacks

Vital to the craft of embracing disappointment is the development of a development outlook, a psychological structure that considers difficulties and disappointments to be open doors for learning and improvement.

A growth mindset recognizes that intelligence and abilities can be improved through effort, practice, and persistence. By reevaluating disappointments as venturing stones on the way to dominance, we make ready for versatility and progress.

A willingness to reflect on experiences with curiosity and an open mind is necessary for learning from setbacks. It involves taking apart disappointments to remove examples, understanding what turned out badly, and planning systems for development. We transform failure into a springboard for future success by going through this process. We do this by dismantling the idea of failure as the final sentence.

Disappointment Flexibility: Building Profound Strength

Disappointment frequently conveys a profound weight that can challenge our psychological and close-to-home prosperity. Building disappointment flexibility is a fundamental ability in exploring the fierce waters of misfortunes. It entails developing the emotional fortitude to withstand failure's blows without giving in to despair or self-doubt.

Versatility is developed through self-empathy, mindfulness, and a sound portion of the point of view. Recognizing that disappointment is a widespread encounter one that even the most achieved people have experienced standardises the cycle. By embracing disappointment as an inescapable piece of the excursion, we strengthen ourselves against the profound cost it can take.

Moving Models: Accounts of Progress Brought into the World from Failure

From the beginning of time, the records of human accomplishment are packed with accounts of people who transformed disappointment into a platform for surprising achievement.

From creators and business visionaries to specialists and competitors, these accounts act as signals of motivation. They remind us that failure is just a bump in the road to greatness rather than the end of the road.

Investigating these accounts, we track down consistent ideas of tirelessness, strength, and relentless confidence in one's vision. The stories of the people who confronted misfortunes, dismissal, and rout, just to arise more grounded and not set in stone, impart in us the mental fortitude to embrace disappointment as a characteristic piece of the cycle.

Their processes enlighten the groundbreaking force of disappointment when met with a versatile soul and an unflinching obligation to development.

As we dive into the core of embracing disappointment, we leave on an excursion that rises above dread and vulnerability. We can harness failure as a potent force in our pursuit of meaningful accomplishment by developing a growth mindset, emotional resilience, and inspiration from those who have gone before us.

Chapter 5

Moving Points of View on Success

In a world frequently characterised by customary benchmarks of accomplishment, this section welcomes us to step outside the limits of regular measurements and set out on an excursion of reclassifying achievement. We will investigate the essential job of exertion and perseverance in chasing objectives, and how adjusting our activities to our guiding principle can prompt a significant feeling of satisfaction and reason.

Past Customary Measurements: Reevaluating Achievement

The scene of achievement is spotted with society's customary markers - awards, abundance, and status. However, these metrics frequently fail to adequately capture the essence of a life that is satisfying and meaningful. Reevaluating accomplishment includes a change in center, from outer approval to natural happiness.

It asks us to think about the quality of our experiences, how we influence others, and the growth and learning that come from our pursuits.

By extending our meaning of progress, we make the way for an additional different and comprehensive point of view. We recognize that the quest for satisfaction isn't inseparable from the quest for outer prizes. This change paves the way for a journey that is more genuine and enriching and encourages us to investigate what truly matters to us.

The Job of Exertion and Determination in Accomplishing Goals

While the charm of moment satisfaction might be enticing, genuine achievement frequently rises out of the pot of exertion and steadiness. The way to progress is seldom direct, and difficulties and difficulties are a vital part of the excursion. Regardless of the challenges we face, the constant companions that propel us forward are effort and perseverance.

Our perception of setbacks is reframed once we realize the significance of effort and perseverance. As opposed to surveying them as disappointments, we remember them as fundamental stages during the time spent in development. Each endeavour, regardless of whether it yields the ideal result, adds to our turn of events and carries us nearer to our objectives.

Tracking down Satisfaction: Aligning Our Actions with Our Values

Amid the noise of external expectations, our values are the compass that leads us toward genuine fulfillment. A harmonious synergy that infuses our endeavors with purpose and passion is created when our actions are in line with our fundamental values. We are on a path of authenticity and integrity when our pursuits are based on what truly moves us.

The quest for an arrangement with our qualities enables us to settle on decisions that reverberate profoundly with our identity. It permits us to explore the bunch of choices we face with clearness and expectation. We tap into a source of motivation and a reservoir of inner satisfaction that transcends fleeting external recognition as we strive to align our actions with our values.

In the impending part, we will dig into the complexities of making an activity-situated attitude, investigating care rehearsals, objective setting procedures, and the specialty of venturing out. As we keep on moving our points of view on progress, we reveal the groundbreaking force of carrying on with a day-to-day existence directed by reason, exertion, and arrangement with our guiding principle.

Chapter 6

Creating an Activity-Situated Mindset

In a world plentiful with yearnings, dreams, and goals, the extension of thought and activity is frequently subtle. This section is a manual for creating an activity situated with a viewpoint that changes the latency of examination into the energy of accomplishment.
We will investigate the specialty of care, the adequacy of defining sensible objectives, and methodologies for beating the inactivity that frequently goes with the initial step.

Methods for Mindfulness: Overseeing Nervousness and Conquering Overthinking

The psyche, a maze of contemplations, can be both a partner and an obstruction in the excursion of transforming desires into the real world. Care rehearses offer the compass to explore the frequently turbulent ocean of tension and overthinking. Mindfulness gives us the clarity to know which thoughts are productive and which are just distractions by grounding us in the now.

In the mission for an activity-situated attitude, care gives the space to stop, assess, and divert our concentration. A device helps with dealing with the incapacitating grasp of vulnerability, encouraging a quiet community from which we can simply decide and make a move.

Determining Achievable Objectives: The SMART Method

Our goals serve as our compass, while our dreams are our coordinates. The Brilliant methodology Explicit, Quantifiable, Feasible, Pertinent, and Time-Bound offers a system for laying out objectives that are both moving and achievable. We break down the path to success into steps that can be taken by transforming vague desires into tangible goals.

The Brilliant methodology tempers aspiration with authenticity, guaranteeing that our objectives are reachable while as yet extending our abilities. We develop a sense of direction that motivates us to move forward with deliberate intent as we align our goals with this structured framework.

The Very First Step: Strategies for Taking Action

The inertia that typically comes before taking action can be a formidable foe. Venturing out requires an essential methodology that sidesteps the obstruction and beats the gravitational draw of inaction. Secured in social brain research, systems, for example, the Two Minute Rule and the Zeigarnik Impact gain by the energy that comes from starting an errand.

Separating undertakings into more modest, reasonable parts evades the overpowering that can prompt hesitation. By zeroing in on the commencement as opposed to the fruition, we prime our brains for activity, actually destroying the obstructions that stand between goal and execution.

We move from being passive observers to active participants in the story of our own lives as we adopt an action-oriented mindset. This transformation is built on mindfulness practices, setting attainable goals, and initiating strategic actions. In the sections that follow, we will explore the difficulties of mishaps and diligence, equipped with an engaged attitude that impels us toward significant achievement.

Chapter 7

Creating a Proactive Action Plan

At the end of our journey, we arrive at the crucial point in the process of creating a proactive action plan, which is a blueprint that shows how to bring an idea into reality. We will investigate the strategic creation of a plan to overcome inaction, the cultivation of habits that maintain our momentum toward meaningful achievement, and the identification of personal triggers that impede progress in this chapter.

Determining Your Triggers: Dread, Compulsiveness, and Procrastination

To graph a course toward proactive activity, we should initially enlighten the shadows cast by our triggers. Dread, frequently the impetus for inaction, can take many structures - anxiety toward disappointment, apprehension about the obscure, or even a feeling of dread toward progress.

Our efforts can be paralyzed before they even begin due to perfectionism's relentless pursuit of perfection. The urge to put things off, or procrastination, can lead us off the path we've chosen.

We dismantle their influence over us by locating these triggers. Mindfulness turns into our safeguard against their impact, permitting us to perceive when they emerge and pick an alternate course. The first step toward regaining control over our actions is recognizing our triggers.

Planning Your Guide: Moves Toward Defeating Inaction

A guide is more than a course; a masterful course of action guides us through the maze of difficulties. Planning this guide includes a conscious cycle that combines aim with methodology. It requires setting clear achievements, separating overall objectives into significant assignments, and framing the assets expected to explore the excursion.

Our guide is not an inflexible outline, but an adaptable aide that adjusts to unexpected exciting bends in the road. By imagining our way and making an organized arrangement, we arm ourselves with the devices expected to explore the unavoidable obstacles and impediments that emerge en route.

Developing Consistency: Propensities for Supported Progress

As predictable animals, our activities are frequently guided by schedules that shape our day-to-day routines. To moor our proactive activity plan, we should develop propensities that advance supported progress. The foundation upon which we construct the structure of success is consistency.

The development of propensities requires goal and redundancy. By beginning little and continuously extending our endeavours, we inject our activities with the force of schedule. After some time, these propensities become natural, changing the quest for progress from an inconsistent undertaking into an indispensable piece of our character.

In the last section of our investigation, we will ponder the groundbreaking excursion we've attempted from grasping the apprehension about disappointment and exposing the fantasy of hairsplitting to embracing disappointment and moving points of view on progress. Outfitted with an activity-situated mentality, directed by a vital guide, and filled with reliable propensities, we stand at the slope of significant achievement and individual satisfaction.

Chapter 8

Staying on Track and Overcoming Obstacles

The road to meaningful accomplishment is rarely straight; an excursion winds through pinnacles and valleys, wins and misfortunes. This chapter explores the art of continuous improvement and provides support through mentorship and community as well as a handbook for developing resilience in the face of adversity. It also provides a guide for navigating the challenges that are bound to come your way.

Perseverance in the Face of Obstacles: Adapting to Unexpected Results

Just like unanticipated storms, challenges can alter our course. However, inside the core of difficulty lies a chance for flexibility to arise. Resilience is more than just getting back up; it's the specialty of adjusting and changing our sails to explore even the most unpleasant waters.

We learn to shift our perspective from defeat to learning when confronted with unexpected outcomes. We embrace mishaps as opportunities to brace our purpose, recalibrate our methodologies, and arise more grounded and savvier. When we are resilient, it becomes a light that guides us forward, even when the way is unclear.

Gaining from Mix-ups

Mistakes, which are frequently misunderstood as detours, are, in fact, necessary for the journey. To master the art of continuous improvement, one must be willing to learn from mistakes and view them as steps toward mastery. Each disappointment, each off-base turn, turns into an important information point that illuminates our future choices.

Recognizing that success is not static is an essential part of adopting a mindset of continuous improvement. A powerful cycle flourishes with transformation, filled with the bits of knowledge acquired from our encounters. We gain the ability to take our endeavors to new heights when we turn setbacks into stepping stones.

Looking for Help: The Importance of Mentorship and Community

We are not solitary explorers in the pursuit of meaningful achievement; rather, we are members of a vast and interconnected world. Mentorship and local areas furnish us with important assets that assist us with exploring difficulties and support our advancement. A coach's direction offers insight into involvement, a compass that guides us through unknown regions.

Local area, then again, goes about as a mainstay of help, a wellspring of consolation, and a mirror that mirrors our advancement. Amid vulnerability, the aggregate insight and shared encounters of a local area can give comfort and motivation. The job of mentorship and the local area can't be put into words in that frame of mind to remain on track and face the hardships.

As we come to the end of this life-altering journey, we reflect on the sections that led us from comprehending the fear of failure to accepting setbacks and seeking support. Outfitted with an activity-situated mentality, sustained by versatility, and floated by the strength of a strong organization, we stand at the edge of understanding our yearnings and embracing an existence of direction, development, and satisfaction.

CONCLUSION

The excursion we've left upon has been a journey of self-revelation, development, and change. From disentangling the complicated strings of dread, hairsplitting, and hesitation to making an activity-situated mentality and exploring misfortunes, we've investigated the complex scene of human potential and the influence of embracing activity. Let us reflect on the profound insights that have illuminated our path as we come to the end of this investigation and anticipate the transformative journey that lies ahead.

Accepting Imperfective Behavior: Your Excursion Ahead

In a world that frequently requests perfect results, we have come to comprehend that flaw isn't a characteristic of disappointment but an identification of genuineness. The quest for hairsplitting has given way to the quest for progress, and the apprehension about disappointment has been changed into the boldness to learn and advance.

Keep in mind that the journey doesn't end when you leave these pages. Embracing blemished activity isn't an objective yet an interminable condition of development. Your process is extraordinarily yours, and one unfurls bit by bit, decision by decision. You are equipped with the knowledge and insights gained to overcome obstacles, overcome setbacks, and seize the numerous opportunities that lie ahead.

Rewarding Achievement: The Transformative Power of Taking Action

You will experience the transformative power of taking action with each step you take, each goal you reach, and each obstacle you overcome. The dormancy of inaction has been supplanted by the invigorating force of progress. You have entered the realm of creation and left the confines of contemplation.

Keep in mind that every action you take adds to the story of your journey as you celebrate your progress, whether it's a big milestone or a small one. The mental fortitude to make a defective move has opened ways to new skylines, disclosing a world rich with potential and probability.

In the orchestra of life, your activities form the tunes that reverberate through time. Your unique masterpiece is made possible by the harmonious combination of each note and chord. Your journey exemplifies the resilience of the human heart, the boundless capacity for development, and the power of the human spirit.

As you close this section and step into the unknown landscape of your future, may your activities be directed by reason, powered by energy, and established in the unshakeable conviction that embracing activity defective, bona fide, and groundbreaking is the way to opening the uncommon potential that lives inside you.

 Your journey is only beginning.
The material is yours to paint, the way is yours to manufacture, and the story is yours to compose. Embrace it with great affection, commend each forward-moving step, and let the extraordinary force of making a move guide you to levels yet inconspicuous.

www.ingramcontent.com/pod-product-compliance
Lightning Source LLC
Chambersburg PA
CBHW060912260726
48661CB00008B/3594